The Best Colle
From Down South

By Derek D. Williams

To Logan
God bless,
From Grandamama ☺
Happy birthday!

November 17, 2025

("The best are the Bobby Bowden
quotes ☺)
(and "Bear" Bryant)

The Best College Football Quotes from Down South

Copyright © 2013 Derek D. Williams

Published: September 3, 2013

This book is dedicated to the greatest sports fans on earth,
Down South in Dixieland.

Table of Contents

OPENING KICKOFF

This is a celebration of the greatest sport in America and the mighty Southeastern Conference. With seven straight national championships as of publication in September 2013, the SEC is unquestionably the most dominant conference in the most beloved sport in America, and is home to the planet's most passionate sports fans.

This book contains the most memorable, hilarious, inspirational and motivational quotes in the history of college football Down South, up through 2013 SEC Media Days. It features a cast of over a hundred characters: coaches, players, announcers and journalists.

Poring over the words of brilliant coaches and incredible players to compile the best quotes was an incredibly rewarding experience. I will feel blessed and humbled if the words contained within this book serve to motivate, educate, inspire or bring a smile to the face of just one reader.

If you have any corrections, or additions you would like to see in future editions, please contact us at collegefootballquotes@gmail.com or visit us at CollegeFootballQuotes.com.

I truly hope you enjoy reading this collection of the greatest college football quotes from Down South!

- Derek D. Williams

University of Tennessee, M.S. 1995

FOOTBALL DOWN SOUTH

"Well, the Southeastern Conference season has begun. I have it on good authority that other college football teams around the country will also be playing games this fall."

- Sports Illustrated columnist and NPR contributor Frank Deford in 2012

"The national championship trophy has been in the South so long it has a sunburn."

- Ray Glier, Atlanta-based national journalist and Author

"I don't know when exactly the SEC took over America. I know this is hard to believe, but the epicenter of college football used to be in the Midwest. I'm so old, I can remember when Notre Dame actually mattered, and the real tough players were supposed to come from Western Pennsylvania and Ohio."

- Sports Illustrated columnist and NPR contributor Frank Deford in 2012

"Football mania is still intensifying throughout the South. … Though football is a national game, the ability to play it well is inordinately concentrated in the South."

- John F. Rooney Jr., Oklahoma State professor and author of *Geography of Sports*

"It's easier to win the national championship than the SEC. Ask Nick Saban."

 - Former Florida & current South Carolina coach Steve Spurrier

"In the East, college football is a cultural exercise. On the West Coast, it is a tourist attraction. In the Midwest, it is cannibalism. But in the South, college football is a religion, and every Saturday is a holy day."

- Marino Casem, Alcorn State University professor

"The SEC is a downhill, man on man game, and you gotta line up and play."

- Florida coach Will Muschamp

"They got a little bit different athlete running around out there. Look at their defensive linemen. Standing next to them, walking off the field, they don't look like a lot of the guys we see. That's the common trait."

- Former Oregon and current Philadelphia Eagles coach Chip Kelly

"If you are a fan of Tennessee or Alabama football there are two rules to live by: Don't get married on the third Saturday in October, and try not to die... because in either case, the preacher might not show."

- ESPN college football expert Beano Cook

"Our fans, to say that they are excited about us being in the SEC would be a complete understatement. They've become fanatical about it."

– Missouri coach Gary Pinkel on the Tigers' inaugural season in the SEC

"The girls are prettier, the air is fresher, and the toilet paper's thicker."

- Missouri wide receiver T.J. Moe, when asked about the Tigers moving from the Big 12 to the Southeastern Conference and what he'd heard about the SEC.

"The SEC has moved out into Texas and up into Missouri. Basically, though, the SEC has always been Deep South, plus Kentucky. Kentucky is apparently allowed in the conference so that everybody else but Vanderbilt gets a guaranteed win — plus, Kentucky bourbon can fuel those famous Southern tailgate parties."

- Sports Illustrated columnist and NPR contributor Frank Deford in 2012

"It's a pretty damn hard league."

- Texas A&M coach Kevin Sumlin, when asked by reporters about playing his first SEC West schedule.

"You gotta wear long britches. They don't wear short pants in that league."

- Texas A&M alumnus and former Alabama coach Gene Stallings' message to the Aggies upon joining the SEC.

"Football in the south is one thing. Football at Auburn is something else."

- ABC/ESPN sideline reporter Adrian Karsten

"It is better to give a lick than receive one. If anybody got in my way, I tried to run right through them."

- Auburn running back and Heisman Trophy winner Bo Jackson

"The game demonstrated the superiority of the Southern teams over any aggregation that the damn yankees could send across the Mason and Dixon Line."

- Philadelphia Bulletin sportswriter Charles Israel writing about Alabama's dominating 61-6 win over Syracuse in the 1953 Orange Bowl.

"You can call it a miracle or a legend or whatever you want to... I just know that on that day (September 8, 1990), Brett Favre was larger than life.'"

- Alabama coach Gene Stallings. Favre led the Golden Eagles to dramatic come-from-behind wins over Florida State, Alabama and Tulane.

"I wish I could say that I went in and ran for the winning touchdown, but I did not. I simply stood by in case my team needed me."

- E. King Gill, the legendary symbol of the 'Twelfth Man' tradition at Texas A&M. After the Aggies had suffered a number of first half injuries, A&M coach Dana Bible remembered that Gill, a former football player, was attending the game as a fan up in the pressbox. Bible called him down from the stands, and Gill suited up and stood on the sidelines, ready to play through the rest of the game, which A&M won 22-14. When the game finally ended, E. King Gill was the only man left standing on the sidelines for the Aggies.

"To the fans and everybody in Gator Nation, I'm sorry. I'm extremely sorry. We were hoping for an undefeated season. That was my goal, something Florida has never done here. I promise you one thing, a lot of good will come out of this. You will never see any player in the entire country play as hard as I will play the rest of the season. You will never see someone push the rest of the team as hard as I will push everybody the rest of the season. You will never see a team play harder than we will the rest of the season. God bless."

- Florida quarterback Tim Tebow and "The Promise" to Gator nation on September 27, 2008.

LIFE LESSONS FROM THE LEGENDS OF THE SOUTH

"Don't go to the grave with life unused."

- Florida State coach Bobby Bowden

"You can learn more character on the two-yard line than anywhere else in life."

- LSU coach Paul Dietzel in 1960

"The real make of a man is how he treats people who can do nothing for him."

- Alabama coach Paul "Bear" Bryant

"I'm one of those guys that thinks if you don't have adversity, forget about character. Because your character is going to be developed by how well you handle adversity. Now if you never have adversity, how are you going to develop character."

- Florida State coach Bobby Bowden

"Happiness is not money and it's not fame and it's not power. Those are nice, but they only last a finger snap. Happiness is a good wife, a good family, and good health."

- Florida State coach Bobby Bowden

"I don't know if you can tell a lot, but you can tell something by the way a man shakes your hand. When I get a firm grip or a limp one, I'm thinking something right off the bat."

- Florida State coach Bobby Bowden

"Losing doesn't make me want to quit. It makes me want to fight that much harder."

- Alabama coach Paul "Bear" Bryant

"When you win, nothing hurts."

- Former Alabama quarterback Joe Namath

"Don't cuss. Don't argue with the officials. And don't lose the game."

-- John Heisman, former Auburn coach on his football philosophy

"I have tried to teach them to show class, to have pride, and to display character. I think football, winning games, takes care of itself if you do that."

- Alabama Coach Paul "Bear" Bryant

"Success comes in a lot of ways, but it doesn't come with money and it doesn't come with fame. It comes from having a meaning in your life, doing what you love and being passionate about what you do. That's having a life of success. When you have the ability to do what you love, love what you do and have the ability to impact people. That's having a life of success. That's what having a life of meaning is."

- Florida quarterback and two-time Heisman Trophy winner Tim Tebow

"You ain't gonna get to the top unless you've got a little poise."

- Florida State coach Bobby Bowden

"I always want my players to show class, knock 'em down, pat on the back, and run back to the huddle."

- Alabama Coach Paul "Bear" Bryant

"Don't talk too much. Don't pop off. Don't talk after the game until you cool off."

- Alabama coach Paul "Bear" Bryant

"I also tell them that your education can take you way farther than a football, baseball, track, or basketball will - that's just the bottom line."

- Former Auburn running back and 1985 Heisman Trophy winner Bo Jackson

"If you don't discipline your children, the sheriff's gonna."

- Florida State coach Bobby Bowden

"Discipline is like holding a bird in your hand. If you squeeze too tight, you kill the bird. If you hold it too loose, it flies away."

- Florida State coach Bobby Bowden On coming to FSU:

"I think the most important thing of all for any team is a winning attitude. The coaches must have it. The players must have it. The student body must have it. If you have dedicated players who believe in themselves, you don't need a lot of talent."

- Alabama Coach Paul "Bear" Bryant

"We can't have two standards, one set for the dedicated young men who want to do something ambitious and one set for those who don't."

- Alabama Coach Paul "Bear" Bryant

"There is no sin in not liking to play; it's a mistake for a boy to be there if he doesn't want to."

- Alabama Coach Paul "Bear" Bryant

"The biggest mistake coaches make is taking borderline cases and trying to save them. I'm not talking about grades now, I'm talking about character. I want to know before a boy enrolls about his home life, and what his parents want him to be."

- Alabama coach Paul "Bear" Bryant

"If a man is a quitter, I'd rather find out in practice than in a game. I ask for all a player has so I'll know later what I can expect."

- Alabama coach Bear Bryant

"The only big games are the ones you lose."

- Florida State coach Bobby Bowden

"When in doubt, punt!"

- Legendary Auburn coach John Heisman, namesake of the most famous trophy in college sports.

"Courage is doing something you need to do that might get you hurt."

- Florida State coach Bobby Bowden

"If somebody mistreats you, treat 'em good. That kills 'em."

- Florida State coach Bobby Bowden

"Like many athletes, I played in college for the chance to play in the pros. In the years since I retired, I've come to realize that the education I got in college was for life. I will have it forever and for that I am incredibly grateful."

- Former Vanderbilt defensive end Pat Toomay

FUNNIEST QUOTES FROM SEC COUNTRY

"But the real tragedy was that 15 hadn't been colored yet."

- Florida coach Steve Spurrier addressing a group of Gator boosters in 1991 by telling them that a fire had broken out at Auburn University's football dorm, which resulted in 20 books burning.

"No man, I majored in Journalism, it was easier."

- Alabama quarterback Joe Namath responding to a journalist who asked him if he majored in Basket Weaving at Alabama.

"I'm glad we're not going to the Gator Bowl."

- Arkansas coach Lou Holtz on being pelted with oranges by Razorback fans towards the end of the game as Arkansas clinched a berth in the Orange Bowl

"He doesn't know the meaning of the word 'fear.' In fact, I just saw his grades, and he doesn't know the meaning of a lot of words."

- Florida State coach Bobby Bowden on coaching Seminoles linebacker Reggie Herring

"He's running the wrong way. Let's see how far he can go."

- Georgia Tech head coach Bill Alexander in the 1929 Rose Bowl. The Yellow Jackets were playing California when midway through the second quarter, Cal's Roy Riegels, who played center, picked up a fumble by Georgia Tech's Jack "Stumpy" Thomason. Although Reigels was only 30 yards away from the Georgia Tech end zone, he was somehow turned around and ran 65 yards in the opposite direction. Cal quarterback Benny Lom chased Riegels from behind, screaming at him to stop running. Lom finally caught up with Riegels at California's 3-yard line and tried to turn him around, but he was immediately gang tackled by a wave of Yellow Jacket players and downed at the one yard line.

"If my mother put on a helmet and shoulder pads and a uniform that wasn't the same as the one I was wearing, I'd run over her if she was in my way. And I love my mother."

- Auburn running back and 1985 Heisman Trophy winner Bo Jackson

"Gentlemen, it is better to have died a small boy than to fumble this football."

- Auburn coach and namesake of the most famous trophy in collegiate sports, John Heisman

"At Georgia Southern, we don't cheat. That costs money, and we don't have any."

 - Georgia Southern coach Erik Russell

"If it was, Army and Navy would be playing for the national championship every year."

- Florida State coach Bobby Bowden when asked whether discipline was the key to winning

"You go by that and they'll have to fire us all."

- Auburn coach Shug Jordan on finding out that LSU coach Charlie McLendon had been fired for not being able to defeat Alabama coach Paul "Bear" Bryant.

"Show me a football coach who shoots good golf and I'll show you a horse s--- coach."

- Alabama coach Paul "Bear" Bryant

"When Herschel Walker was here, tweeting was a sound a bird made. The definition of media is a lot different than today. Just go back. There was no Internet. No cell phones. … There was not talk radio."

- Georgia senior associate athletic director Claude Felton on the media landscape in 2013

"I don't know what e-mail looks like. The Internet? Don't know what it is. Maybe if I retired I'd have time to learn."

- Florida State coach Bobby Bowden

"I don't know why they call it a hash tag I call it a number sign #makesnosense"

– Tweet from Florida coach Will Muschamp [@CoachWMuschamp] on May 8, 2013

"If Steve Spurrier were coming over for dinner, what would I cook for him? Nothin'. I don't cook. I don't cook cereal. Not even cold cereal. I'm tellin' ya, I don't cook nothin'! I might take him out to a good restaurant, though."

- Florida State coach Bobby Bowden on his former arch nemesis Florida coach Steve Spurrier

"He's a good coach, but I'd like to run into him some night down a dark alley."

- Georgia Ray Goff talking about Florida coach Steve Spurrier

"The definition of an atheist in Alabama is someone who doesn't believe in Bear Bryant."

- Georgia coach Wally Butts on his greatest nemesis, Alabama Coach Bear Bryant

"I was so poor that I had a tumbleweed as a pet."

- Texas coach Darrell K Royal

"This is the greatest football state in America. It's a place where the women understand what it means and how to play it."

- LSU coach Les Miles talking about the state of Louisiana and its female residents on October 7, 2009

"If he doesn't win the Heisman, that should be investigated. That will be the biggest ripoff since we stole everything from the Indians."

- NBA Hall of Famer and Auburn alumnus Charles Barkley on what would happen if Cam Newton didn't win the 2010 Heisman Trophy

"Always remember... Goliath was a 40 point favorite over David."

- Auburn coach Shug Jordan

"No, but you can see it from here."

- Arkansas coach Lou Holtz when asked if Fayetteville was the end of the world.

"In my experience I've learned women are better streakers."

- Florida coach Steve Spurrier when asked to comment on a streaker who ran onto the field.

"Here's a twenty, bury two."

- Coach Bear Bryant upon being asked to contribute ten dollars to help cover the cost of a sportswriter's funeral.

"When I went to Tennessee, I could name you every quarterback in the SEC for the last 20 years. We had to teach Eli the 12 teams in the SEC before he went to Ole Miss."

- Former Tennessee quarterback Peyton Manning speaking about his brother, former Ole Miss quarterback Eli Manning

"Sixty Minutes."

- Auburn coach Pat Dye's response to the question 'How long will it take you to beat Alabama?'

"I'd also like to make a note here that in the last 21 seasons, you as the media have only picked the right team four times to win the SEC. Now, if I was 4-17 as a coach, I would be back in West Virginia pumping my gas at my daddy's gas station, which we don't really want to go there."

- Coach Nick Saban on the Crimson Tide being picked to win the SEC again in 2013.

"Son, you've got a good engine, but your hands aren't on the steering wheel."

- Florida State coach Bobby Bowden

"I'm so far in debt that I'll never get out of it, so I might as well be in debt where it's warm."

- Texas coach Darrell K Royal addressing the rumor that he was going to take a coaching job with the New York Giants.

 "If you're a youngster in Alabama, start getting the football out and throw it around the backyard with pop!"

- ESPN television announcer Brent Musburger's suggestion to the youth of Alabama after verbally drooling over Alabama quarterback A.J. McCarron's girlfriend Katherine Webb during the 2013 BCS Championship, turning Webb into a Twitter sensation and overnight celebrity.

"Baseball and football are very different games. In a way, both of them are easy. Football is easy if you're crazy as hell. Baseball is easy if you've got patience. They'd both be easier for me if I were a little more crazy… and a little more patient."

- Former Auburn running back and 1985 Heisman Trophy winner Bo Jackson

"Trust me, we're playing the smart kids this week. If you can't beat the smart kids, you're in for a long year."

- NBA Hall of Famer and Auburn alumnus Charles Barkley when asked about Auburn's upcoming game against Vanderbilt

"My advice to defensive players: Take the shortest route to the ball and arrive in a bad humor."

- Tennessee coach Bowden Wyatt

"We're in the SEC. Seriously - you know what y'all call SMU? They'da fit in fine in the SEC. Texas and Oklahoma just hated them. But in the SEC, dude, we'll make sure you're well taken care of. Everyone wants to give us a hard time about giving Cam Newton two hundred K. That's called a good damn investment. We got him for two hundred grand? Are you kidding me? On the good days, I wish my accountant could do stuff like that."

- Auburn alumnus and NBA Hall of Famer Charles Barkley on Heisman Trophy and national championship winning quarterback Cam Newton.

CLASSIC DIXIELAND INSULTS

"You can't spell Citrus without UT"

- Florida coach Steve Spurrier on Tennessee playing in the Citrus Bowl, which is the designated bowl for the second-choice team from the SEC.

"What do the moon and Texas A&M have in common? They both control the Tide."

- Texas A&M Athletic Director Eric Hyman speaking to boosters during the 2013 offseason after the Aggies and Johnny "Football" Manziel had defeated Alabama the previous fall.

"Well Eli, Smokey just came out of the tunnel, and he's about 100 yards away from me now - and if I had my deer rifle, I believe I could drop him. Back to you, Eli."

- Crimson Tide football network sideline reporter Jerry Duncan's comments to radio voice Eli Gold just prior to kickoff in a game against Tennessee.

"In Alabama, there are three classes of people: Alabama fans, Auburn Tiger fans, and atheists. Two of the three will go to Hades when they die. Which two depends entirely on who you ask."

- Author David Shepard in *Bama, Bear Bryant and the Bible*

"If someone in Los Angeles asks you and you say 'I played at Alabama,' everyone knows what that means. If you had to say 'I played at Auburn,' that would be about like saying 'I played at Rutgers.' People aren't even sure where it is."

- Leon Douglas, former University of Alabama basketball center (1972–1976) and current men's basketball coach at Tuskegee University.

"The first person I would like to thank is the good Lord, for giving me the ability to play the game of football; because without the ability to play the game, I would have been at Auburn."

- Former Alabama defensive tackle Marty Lyons (1975-1978)

"The day Elvis died, the day Michael Jackson died, and the day Mike Shula got fired."

- NBA Hall of Famer and Auburn alumnus Charles Barkley on the three saddest days in his life. Auburn had a four year winning streak against Alabama when Mike Shula was head coach of the Crimson Tide from 2003 to 2006.

"Free Shoes University"

- According to Florida coach Steve Spurrier, this is what the letters FSU stand for; the statement was made following the suspension of several Florida State players for accepting free sneakers.

"What's the matter, honey, don't you people take football seriously?"

- Alabama coach Paul "Bear" Bryant after calling the Auburn football offices at 7 a.m. and hearing from the female receptionist that none of the coaches were in their offices yet.

"Everybody thought that was a nice joke, but I meant it. You can get the Auburn people now at 7:00, or thereabouts, because they've been trying harder."

- Alabama coach Paul "Bear" Bryant on his aforementioned phone call to the Auburn football staff.

"I don't know. I sort of always liked playing them that second game because you could always count on them having two or three key players suspended."

- South Carolina coach Steve Spurrier offering his candid opinion on the Georgia vs. South Carolina game moving from the traditional second week of the season to the sixth week in 2012.

"Why? I've got a better record on that field than he does".

- Duke coach Steve Spurrier's response to North Carolina coach Mack Brown's statement that Spurrier had shown a real lack of class by bringing his Blue Devils team back onto the field to take photos with the scoreboard in the background. Brown told the media that Spurrier shouldn't be pulling that maneuver on someone else's home field.

"I thought this was Vanderbilt country."

- South Carolina coach Steve Spurrier when asked by Tennessee media how he felt being in "Big Orange" country.

"Sure I'd like to beat Notre Dame, don't get me wrong. But nothing matters more than beating that cow college on the other side of the state."

- Alabama coach Paul "Bear" Bryant addressing a group of Alabama boosters before an Iron Bowl game against the Tigers.

"How come they get to pretend they are soldiers? The thing is, they aren't actually in the military. I ought to have Mike's Pirate School. The freshmen, all they get is bandanas. When you're a senior, you get the sword and skull and crossbones. For homework, we'll work on pirate maneuvers and stuff like that."

- Former Texas Tech coach Mike Leach on the cadet corps at Texas A&M

"I know why Peyton came back for his senior year: he wanted to be a three-time Citrus Bowl MVP."

- Florida coach Steve Spurrier discussing quarterback Peyton Manning's decision to return to Tennessee for his senior year

"Tell Mr. Sunseri at Alabama, don't worry. He's going to get to spend lots of quality time with his dad in about six games."

- NBA Hall of Famer and Auburn alumnus Charles Barkley after being shown a clip of Vinnie Sunseri, Alabama's safety, talking about playing against his dad, Tennessee's defensive coordinator, Sal Sunseri. The younger Sunseri said he was looking forward to seeing his dad again, whose Tennessee defense was historically horrible in 2012. Sal Sunseri was later fired at the end of the 2012 season.

"If he'd kicked it straight, we would have blocked it."

- Coach Bear Bryant talking about Tennessee's missed field goal in the last minute of a 1966 game in Knoxville, which was won by Alabama 11-10 after trailing the Volunteers by ten points in the fourth quarter. The win preserved Alabama's undefeated season.

BEAR BRYANT AND ALABAMA

"And believe me, to have been in the city of Tuscaloosa in October when you were young and full of Early Times and had a shining Alabama girl by your side--to have had all that and then to have seen those red shirts pour onto the field, and, then, coming behind them, with that inexorable big cat walk of his, the man himself, The Bear--that was very good indeed."

- Howell Raines, executive editor of the New York Times, who received his master's degree in English from the University of Alabama, along with an honorary doctorate from UA in 1993.

"His nickname was Bear. Now imagine a guy that can carry the nickname Bear."

- Former Alabama Quarterback Joe Namath

"I don't know, we haven't played Alabama yet."

- Legendary Green Bay head coach Vince Lombardi responding to a reporter's question on what it felt like to have the world's greatest football team for the season right after his Packers won Super Bowl I on January 15, 1967. This quote is even more profound when you consider the 1966 Alabama Crimson Tide football team finished third in the polls despite going undefeated, winning the SEC and defeating Big 8 champions Nebraska 34-7 in the 1967 Sugar Bowl.

"Whenever I see those crimson jerseys and crimson helmets, I feel humbled to have played football for Alabama. Other players in the NFL talk to me about their schools and their traditions. I just smile knowing the immense love Alabama fans have for our school and its football program. I'm proud to be a part of that Crimson Tide heritage."

- Former Alabama All-America linebacker Derrick Thomas

"I thought Nebraska was the most football-crazed state until I came to Alabama. Coach Bryant got up and introduced members of the 1925 Rose Bowl team, and he got teary-eyed, and so did all the people in the audience who welcomed the team with an absolute admiration that is hard to describe."

- Author James Michener in 1975 while writing his book *Sports in America*.

"I can't imagine being in the Hall of Fame with Coach Bryant. There ought to be two Hall of Fames, one for Coach Bryant and one for everybody else."

- Former Crimson Tide tight end and current Baltimore Ravens GM Ozzie Newsome, upon his induction to the Alabama Hall of Fame.

"I don't know about the rest of you, but I know one thing. Ol' thirty-four will be after them. He'll be after their asses!"

- Former Alabama coach Hank Crisp speaking about his starting end, a second-team All-SEC player by the name of Paul William "Bear" Bryant, before a 1935 game between the Crimson Tide and

Tennessee. Bryant had a fractured bone in his leg and was not expected to play in the game. During the pregame locker room speech, Bryant decided he must play, and had one of the best games of his career on a partially broken leg.

"You never know what a football player is made of until he plays against Alabama."

- Tennessee coach General Robert Neyland

"His ear had a real nasty cut and it was dangling from his head, bleeding badly. He grabbed his own ear and tried to yank it from his head. His teammates stopped him and the managers bandaged him. Man was that guy a tough one. He wanted to tear off his own ear so he could keep playing."

- Tennessee lineman Bull Bayer talking about his Alabama counterpart in the trenches, All-American Bully VandeGraaf in the 1913 Alabama vs. Tennessee game

"The expectation level is high at the University of Alabama and it should be. What's wrong with people expecting excellence?"

- Alabama coach Gene Stallings upon being hired as head coach of the Crimson Tide in 1990

"I grew up sneaking into Legion Field to see Alabama play. I vividly remember Joe Namath's first varsity game. I remember Kenny Stabler running down the sideline in the rain and mud against Auburn. I remember Lee Roy Jordan chasing down a

running back and intimidating without even hitting. I really appreciate the people who have contributed to this legacy and the tradition that has been passed down. And the people who have continued it--the goal line stand and Van Tiffin's kick and all those memories of people who have carried on the tradition of Alabama football. I really feel blessed to have had the opportunity to be part of the tradition of Alabama football."

- Former Alabama All-American running back Johnny Musso

"We don't talk about winning championships, we talk about being champions."

- Alabama coach Nick Saban

"They talk about the Alabama family not being reasonable and realistic. Well hell no, we're not supposed to be reasonable and realistic. We're Alabama -- we're supposed to be the best."

- Former Alabama Quarterback Kenny Stabler

"If I could reach my students like that, I'd teach for nothing."

- An Alabama professor after observing the reactions of players to a pregame talk by Coach Paul W. "Bear" Bryant.

"I guess I'm just too full of Bama."

- Former Alabama fullback Tommy Lewis, explaining why he charged off the bench without a helmet to tackle Rice's halfback

Dickey Moegle, who was on his way to a 95 yard touchdown run in the 1954 Cotton Bowl.

"I don't know if I'll ever get tired of football. One time I thought I might. . . I was out there on the practice field wondering whether football had passed me by. Then I heard the Million Dollar Band playing over on the practice field. When they started playing 'Yea, Alabama,' I got goosebumps all over me. I looked out there and those young rascals in those crimson jerseys, and I just wanted to thank God for giving me the opportunity to coach and contribute in some small way at my alma mater and be a part of the University of Alabama tradition."

- Coach Bear Bryant when asked whether he would ever get tired of coaching football

"Coach Bryant always taught us we were special and never to accept being ordinary. I think that is one thing that has sustained Alabama through the years. Players with ordinary ability feeling somehow, someway they would find it within themselves to make a play to help Alabama win a football game. There is no way to describe the pride an Alabama player feels in himself and the tradition of the school."

- Former Alabama quarterback Kenny Stabler

"Everyone says we can't beat Miami, but we are not just anybody, we are Alabama."

- Former Alabama quarterback David Palmer just before the 1992 Sugar Bowl.

"What are you doing here? Tell me why you are here. If you are not here to win a national championship, you're in the wrong place. You boys are special. I don't want my players to be like other students. I want special people. You can learn a lot on the football field that isn't taught in the home, the church, or the classroom. There are going to be days when you think you've got no more to give and then you're going to give plenty more. You are going to have pride and class. You are going to be very special. You are going to win the national championship for Alabama."

- Coach Bear Bryant

"I left Texas A&M because my school called me. Mama called, and when Mama calls, then you just have to come running."

- Coach Bear Bryant on why he left Texas A&M with six years left on his contract to become head coach of Alabama in 1958.

"I make my practices real hard because if a player is a quitter, I want him to quit in practice, not in a game."

- Alabama coach Paul "Bear" Bryant

"Wasn't anything for us to stay three or four hours. People'd be dropping like flies, they'd tote 'em off the field, pack 'em in ice,

give 'em some water and the next day they'd have to be right back out there. I think Coach Bryant was lucky no one died."

- Former Alabama tackle Jerry Duncan on the brutal practices under Coach Bryant

"All I know is that we went out there in two buses and we came back in one."

- Former Texas A&M player and one of the Junction Boys, Gene Stallings, upon being asked if Coach Paul "Bear" Bryant's first practices at Texas A&M were as tough as reported. Stallings was one of the players who survived Coach Bryant's legendarily brutal 10 day summer football camp in Junction, Texas in September 1954. There were nearly 100 players on the two buses that headed for Junction on September 1st. One bus with 35 players arrived back in College Station on September 10th. Stallings served as Alabama head coach from 1990 to 1996.

"Woody is a great coach . . . and I ain't bad."

- Alabama coach Paul Bear Bryant after the Crimson Tide defeated Woody Hayes and the Ohio State Buckeyes 35 - 6 in the 1978 Sugar Bowl.

"I have always tried to teach my players to be fighters. When I say that, I don't mean put up your dukes and get in a fistfight over something. I'm talking about facing adversity in your life. There is not a person alive who isn't going to have some awfully bad days in their lives. I tell my players that what I mean by fighting is when your house burns down, and your wife runs off

with the drummer, and you've lost your job and all the odds are against you. What are you going to do? Most people just lay down and quit. Well, I want my people to fight back."

- Alabama coach Paul "Bear" Bryant

"If you want to walk the heavenly streets of gold, you gotta know the password, "Roll, Tide, Roll!"

- Alabama coach Paul "Bear" Bryant

THE BEST OF STEVE SPURRIER

"I prefer, and my friends often refer to me as the HBC or Head Ball Coach. I would appreciate it if you would use Head Ball Coach."

- Former Florida and current South Carolina coach Steve Spurrier

"Surprised? It's Vandy. There must have been something good on TV."

- Florida coach Steve Spurrier when asked if he was surprised at the lackluster attendance for the 1998 Gators game against Vanderbilt in Nashville.

"It was really loud, possibly louder than the swamp. Then the game started."

- Florida coach Steve Spurrier when asked at halftime if Tennessee's 102,000+ seat Neyland Stadium was the loudest place he had ever played in.

"Danny Wuerffel is a New Testament guy. You slap him upside the helmet, and he'll turn the other cheek.... I'm a little more Old Testament. If you spear our guy in the ear hole, I think we're supposed to be able to spear your guy in the ear hole."

- Steve Spurrier questioning perceived late hits by Florida State Seminoles defenders on his quarterback.

"My dad was a preacher. He never lasted 10, 12 years anywhere. So every few years we'd move, guess they'd already heard all of his sermons."

- Former Florida and current South Carolina coach Steve Spurrier on why so many coaches move around in the SEC

"The Pope is 77 and can lead a million people. I only have to get 11 players on the field."

- South Carolina coach Steve Spurrier on getting older. Steve Spurrier

"A swamp is where Gators live. We feel comfortable there, but we hope our opponents feel tentative. A swamp is hot and sticky and can be dangerous. Only Gators get out alive."

- Florida coach Steve Spurrier

"So you get two good hours on the field about every day, you get about an hour and a half in the meeting room and that's pretty much all you need to thoroughly coach your team."

- Former Florida coach and current South Carolina coach Steve Spurrier

"If you play close games, you're not going to win them all. Miracles will not continue forever. Somebody asked me if

Tennessee could go 13-0 again and I said, 'If some miracles keep happening for them, sure.' But you can't rely on miracles."

- Florida coach Steve Spurrier on Tennessee's 1998 national championship

"Please don't clap when we lose a game."

- South Carolina coach Steve Spurrier went to South Carolina seven seasons ago, he was disheartened when he heard fans applaud the team after a close loss.

"In my experience I've learned women are better streakers."

- Former Florida coach Steve Spurrier when asked to comment about a streaker on the field

"Is Ray Goff still the head coach there?"

- Florida coach Steve Spurrier when asked by a reporter if Gators would beat Georgia that year. Spurrier had enjoyed several consecutive wins over Goff and the Bulldogs.

"There's one sure way to stop us from scoring - give us the ball near the goal line."

- South Carolina coach Steve Spurrier in 2007 after the Gamecocks lost to Vanderbilt

"Their pass defense was number one in the nation coming in, but it won't be going out."

- Florida coach Steve Spurrier after the Gators defeated Mississippi State 52-0.

"I'm not saying anybody broke any rules; I'm just saying there was a feeling of, well, those kids are driving awfully nice cars. How's it happen?"

- Steve Spurrier, in a 1995 Sports Illustrated article, one year after telling boosters that FSU stood for "Free Shoes University."

"I've always said Spurrier is the best coach since Bryant, and I would have loved to [have] seen them go head to head. I think Spurrier would have had some success, at least more than anyone else did. I really think Spurrier would have driven Bryant crazy."

- ESPN college football host Paul Finebaum

LES MILES IN THE BAYOU

"At LSU, we show up at the stadium, ninety-two thousand five hundred, all figuring LSU is going to win. Just by how much is the question."

- LSU coach Les Miles on July 23, 2010

"No game is won on a twitter page."

- LSU coach Les Miles discussing an pregame argument on twitter between his cornerback Tyrann "Honey Badger" Mathieu and Alabama starting quarterback A.J. McCarron.

"Louisiana has a heritage of great players that play their high school football within the boundaries of Louisiana."

- LSU coach Les Miles on January 2, 2005

"I have a little tradition that humbles me as a man, that lets me know I'm part of the field and part of the field. I can tell you one thing, the grass at Tiger Stadium tastes best."

- LSU coach Les Miles on his habit of plucking a few blades of grass from the field and chewing on it.

"You're not eating. All you're doing is tasting."

- LSU coach Les Miles when pressed further on his grass chewing habit

"When I wake up in the morning and I turn that film on, it's like reading a book, and it's exciting … I don't read books, but if I read books, it would be like reading a book."

- LSU coach Les Miles

"Whether the light switch is on in every room or not, I'm not certain. But I can tell you that most of the house is lit."

- LSU coach Les Miles in *The Times-Picayune* on November 22, 2008 when asked about the improvement shown by one of his players had shown.

"Here are the three spots where the cupboard needs a little improvement for us to do the things that we need to accomplish: One of them is on offense, one of them is on defense and one is special teams."

- LSU coach Les Miles

The SEC > Everyone Else

"At Alabama, we teach our men to win."

- Coach Bear Bryant when asked about Notre Dame coach Ara Parseghian's decision to play for a 10-10 tie against Michigan State with 1:10 left on clock, rather than attempt to win the game. The Fighting Irish and Spartans finished ranked #1 and #2 in the polls with identical 9-0-1 records. Alabama finished third in the final polls, despite going undefeated, winning the SEC regular season title and demolishing Big 8 champions Nebraska 34-7 in the 1967 Sugar Bowl.

"I would like nothing better than to play USC for the title. I can tell you this, that they have a much easier road to travel. They're going to play real knockdown drag-outs with UCLA and Washington, Cal-Berkeley, Stanford -- some real juggernauts -- and they're going to end up, it would be my guess, in some position so if they win a game or two, that they'll end up in the title."

- LSU coach Les Miles on the USC Trojans and their substandard PAC-12 competition in the mid-2000s

"In both situations we were turned in by Ohio. We didn't do anything wrong. The University of Florida didn't do anything wrong. And so we appreciated our friends from Ohio making sure we're compliant with NCAA rules. They certainly know a little bit about that subject."

- Florida coach Will Muschamp was asked about Ohio State turning Florida for two minor recruiting violations at 2013 SEC Media Days.

"He's got a nice little gig going, a little bit like (John) Calipari. He tells guys, 'Hey, three years from now, you're going to be a first-round pick and go.' If he wants to be the greatest coach or one of the greatest coaches in college football, to me, he has to go somewhere besides Alabama and win, because they've always won there at Alabama."

- South Carolina coach Steve Spurrier offers his thoughts on Nick Saban and what he's done at Alabama.

"LSU wasn't winning when I went there. Michigan State wasn't winning when I went there. Toledo wasn't winning when I went there. And Alabama really wasn't winning when I came here. I guess I gotta go someplace else. I don't know. I think it's great, I love Steve. I'm always anxious to hear what he has to say – it's always funny."

- Alabama coach Nick Saban

"That wasn't right. It was a bad deal. And it will forever be in the mind of Urban Meyer and in the mind of our football team. ... And it's going to be a big deal."

- Florida coach Urban Meyer in his book, "Urban's Way," talking about the highly controversial stunt ordered by Georgia coach Mark Richt in the 2007 edition of The World's Largest Cocktail Party. Richt ordered his entire team - meaning every single player on the Georgia sideline – to run out on to the field to celebrate the team's first touchdown. Although the move cost Georgia a 15-yard excessive celebration penalty and drew the scorn of both Florida fans and observers, the tactic worked exactly as Richt hoped it would. Georgia went on to upset Florida, 42-30, adding serious fuel to an already fiery rivalry.

"How well would they have done if they played the six (SEC) teams ranked in the Top 10? Would they beat them all? Would they beat three of them? And I think they have a really good team and Urban (Meyer) is a great coach. I'm not questioning any of that. I'm just saying that's where strength of schedule and who you play don't get sort of accounted for quite equally."

- Alabama coach Nick Saban at 2013 SEC media days, discussing the current BCS system, the Ohio State Buckeyes and their coach Urban Meyer.

"Well, it depends on what gap you're talking about. What are the bottom six doing? So they've had the best team in college football. They haven't had the whole conference. Because, again, half of 'em haven't done much at all. I'm just asking you. You tell me. It depends on who you want to listen to," Stoops said. "Listen, they've had the best team in college football, meaning they've won the national championship. That doesn't mean everything else is always the best."

- Oklahoma coach Bob Stoops May 2013 on Big 12 Conference schools and others around the nation don't have to close some mythical gap with the SEC.

"I'd be saying the same thing if I were in the Big 12. I said it for three years."

- Florida coach Will Muschamp (former defensive coordinator at Texas) after hearing Bob Stoops's comments at 2013 SEC Media Days.

"So you're listening to a lot of propaganda that gets fed out to you. You're more than smart enough to figure it out. Again, you can look at the top two, three, four, five, six teams, and you can look at the bottom six, seven, eight, whatever they are. How well are they all doing? What'd we (the Big 12) have, eight of 10 teams in bowl games this year? Again, you figure it all out."

- Oklahoma coach Bob Stoops

"I've got more important things to do than sit around and read what Bob Stoops has to say about anything."

- Alabama coach Nick Saban commenting on Bob Stoops' quotes about SEC:

HOW DOES THAT CROW TASTE?

"I'm really looking forward to embracing some of the great traditions at the University of Tennessee, for instance the Vol Walk, running through the T, singing Rocky Top all night long after we beat Florida next year, it will be a blast."

- Former Tennessee and current USC head coach Lane Kiffin

"Bullsh*t like tonight is a reason why I can't wait to leave college station… whenever it may be"

- Texas A&M quarterback and 2012 Heisman Trophy winner Johnny Manziel on Twitter during his tumultuous 2013 offseason

"I think the Big Ten, talent-wise, is a lot better, and the defenses in the Big Ten are better than SEC defenses."

- Nebraska quarterback Taylor Martinez a few days before the Huskers took on Georgia in the 2013 Capital One Bowl. The Bulldogs beat the Huskers 45-31 and Martinez threw two interceptions.

"Alabama's cornerbacks don't impress me one bit. They're overrated. Real men don't play zone defense and we'll show them a thing or two come January 1."

- Miami Receiver Lamar Thomas before the 1993 Sugar Bowl. During the game, Alabama defensive back George Teague incredibly ran down Thomas from behind and stripped the ball from his hands, saving a touchdown and providing an enormous momentum shift that propelled the Crimson Tide to a 34-13 victory over the Hurricanes on the way to Alabama's 12th national championship. The play is widely referred to as The Play of the Century.

"We're in the SEC. If you aren't cheatin', you ain't tryin'. We got Alabama, Georgia, Florida…"

- NBA Hall of Famer and Auburn alumnus Charles Barkley in May 2006

"I made this clear to Jeremy Foley (Florida Athletic Director), if I am able to go coach, I want to coach at one place, the University of Florida. It would be a travesty, it would be ridiculous to all of a sudden come back and get the feeling back, get the health back, feel good again and then all of a sudden go throw some other colors on my shirt and go coach? I don't want to do that. I have too much love for this University and these players and for what we've built."

- Former Florida and current Ohio State coach Urban Meyer, after resigning at UF (the first time) and then coming back to coach a day later.

GENERAL NEYLAND AND TENNESSEE

"I've heard everything. I've heard it was because I just wanted to beat Florida or because I wanted to win the Heisman. It's none of those. I love college and I love college football. I just wanted to play one more year and have all those feelings one more time. I don't know why people won't accept that."

- Former Tennessee quarterback and future Hall of Famer Peyton Manning on why he returned to UT for his senior season

"It's a peppy-type deal. Our band plays it at least 20 times a game. Though I'm sure our opponents would put that number close to a hundred."

- Tennessee Sports Information Director Bud Ford on the oft-played song 'Rocky Top'.

"When you throw the ball, three things can happen -- and two of them are bad."

- Tennessee coach General Robert Neyland

"He (General Robert Neyland) doesn't always get credit for the quote, as it is often attributed to Woody Hayes. But it was Neyland."

- ESPN college football commentator Beano Cook

"Almost all close games are lost by the losers, not won by the winners."

- Tennessee coach General Robert Neyland

 "You only get one chance in life to be in college and to play football in this kind of atmosphere. I hope to go and have a good experience as a professional. But I just wasn't ready to give this up. It is just too special."

- Former Tennessee quarterback and future Hall of Famer Peyton Manning

"The Seven Maxims of Football"

1. **The team that makes the fewest mistakes will win.**
2. **Play for and make the breaks and when one comes your way - SCORE.**
3. **If at first the game - or the breaks - go against you, don't let up... put on more steam.**
4. **Protect our kickers, our QB, our lead and our ball game.**
5. **Ball, oskie, cover, block, cut and slice, pursue and gang tackle... for this is the WINNING EDGE.**
6. **Press the kicking game. Here is where the breaks are made.**
7. **Carry the fight to our opponent and keep it there for 60 minutes.**

- Tennessee coach General Robert Neyland

"I probably would have gone to Ole Miss, just to have the opportunity to play with him again, especially at my parents' alma mater...Had my dad told me to go to Ole Miss, I would have gone to Ole Miss. I'm thankful that my dad let me make my own decision."

- Former Tennessee quarterback Peyton Manning on not following his father and older brother Cooper to Ole Miss, if his brother Cooper didn't have to quit football due to a spinal condition.

"Johnny Majors is the most beloved Southerner of all time in Pennsylvania."

- ESPN college football announcer Beano Cook talking about former Tennessee and Pittsburgh coach Johnny Majors, who led the Panthers to the national championship in 1978.

GOOD OL' BOBBY BOWDEN

"When I was at Alabama, all I heard was, 'Beat Auburn.' When I was at West Virginia, all I heard was, 'Beat Pittsburgh.' When I got to Florida State, their bumper stickers read, 'Beat Anybody.'"

- Florida State coach Bobby Bowden on coming to FSU

"You want to know what a real test of faith is? That's when you go to church and reach into your pocket, and all you got is a $20 bill."

- Florida State coach Bobby Bowden

"Why does everyone make such a big deal about "wide right"? If you're gonna miss, you can't be anything but wide right or wide left. It's bound to be one of 'em."

- Florida State coach Bobby Bowden

"I know their mother; she'd give them all my plays."

- Florida State coach Bobby Bowden on why he didn't want to play teams coached by his sons

"When I coached at West Virginia and we began to integrate back in the sixties, white people used to come up to me and say, "How many black guys you got on the team?" I'd say, "I don't know. I don't count." They're all some mama's son to me."

- Florida State coach Bobby Bowden

"They look so good to me. I'm amazed they're not on strike."

- Florida State coach Bobby Bowden after the Seminoles lost to the University of Miami during the 1987 NFL strike

"The good news is our defense is giving up only a touchdown a game. The bad news is our offense is, too."

- Florida State coach Bobby Bowden

"Darkest day of my coaching career in forty-seven years was at my first head-coaching job at a major college -- West Virginia. We played Pitt, the big rival. For those folks, that game is like Florida State-Florida or Auburn-Alabama. You go to coach at West Virginia and you want to make the fans like you, you beat Pitt. We go up there in 1970, and we get ahead, 35-8, at the half. I thought, Just go out there and don't make any mistakes and we got the game won. Well, we go back out and lose, 36-35. Whooooooo! I learned a lot from that loss to Pitt. I've never let it happen again. People get on me for running up the score. Don't care. I'll never sit on the ball again."

- Florida State coach Bobby Bowden

"Routine is imperative in football. Repetition, repetition, repetition. Until it becomes habit, habit, habit."

- Florida State coach Bobby Bowden

"They'll call it nepotism, but half of them don't know how to spell it and the other half doesn't know what it means."

- Florida State coach Bobby Bowden on being criticized for having his sons on the FSU coaching staff.

"The Good Lord might not want to take me, but He might be after the pilot."

- Florida State coach Bobby Bowden on his fear of small planes

"Not if they want to win."

- Florida State coach Bobby Bowden when asked if he thought Oklahoma head coach Bob Stoops and assistant coach Steve Spurrier Jr. would consult Florida coach Steve Spurrier Sr. for tips on how to play FSU in the 2000 Orange Bowl national championship.

"It was self-suicide."

- Florida State coach Bobby Bowden on FSU's seven turnovers and 13 penalties in a loss to Wake Forest.

"As good as we were, we didn't win a National Championship until 1993, mainly because we kept losing to Miami on missed kicks. I used to get mad because nobody else would play Miami. Notre Dame would play them, then drop them. Florida dropped them. Penn State dropped them. We would play Miami and lose by one point on a missed field goal, and it would knock us out of the National Championship. I didn't want to play them, either, but I had to play them. That's why I said, when I die, they'll say, 'At least he played Miami."

- Florida State coach Bobby Bowden

"I guess I'll retire some day, if I live that long."

- Florida State coach Bobby Bowden

"A better ending could not have been scripted. Of course, if we had won, that would have been better."

- Florida State coach Bobby Bowden

"After you retire, there's only one big event left...and I ain't ready for that."

- Florida State coach Bobby Bowden

"Heaven is nothing but good."

- Florida State coach Bobby Bowden

BEAR BRYANT ON COACHING FOOTBALL

"Football has never been just a game to me. Never."

- Alabama Coach Paul "Bear" Bryant

"Mama wanted me to be a preacher. I told her coachin' and preachin' were a lot alike."

- Alabama Coach Paul "Bear" Bryant

"If you want to coach you have three rules to follow to win. One, surround yourself with people who can't live without football. I've had a lot of them. Two, be able to recognize winners. They come in all forms. And, three, have a plan for everything. A plan for practice, a plan for the game. A plan for being ahead, and a plan for being behind 20-0 at half, with your quarterback hurt and the phones dead, with it raining cats and dogs and no rain gear because the equipment man left it at home."

- Alabama Coach Paul "Bear" Bryant

"I'm just a simple plow hand from Arkansas, but I have learned over the years how to hold a team together. How to lift some men up, how to calm others down, until finally they've got one heartbeat, together, a team."

- Alabama Coach Paul "Bear" Bryant when asked why he was so successful as a coach.

"The idea of molding men means a lot to me."

- Coach Bear Bryant

"Don't ever give up on ability. Don't give up on a player who has it."

- Alabama Coach Paul "Bear" Bryant

"People who are in it for their own good are individualists. They don't share the same heartbeat that makes a team so great. A great unit, whether it be football or any organization, shares the same heartbeat."

- Alabama Coach Paul "Bear" Bryant

"I'll never give up on a player regardless of his ability as long as he never gives up on himself. In time he will develop."

- Alabama Coach Paul "Bear" Bryant

"You must learn how to hold a team together. You must lift some men up, calm others down, until finally they've got one heartbeat. Then you've got yourself a team."

- Alabama Coach Paul "Bear" Bryant

"I don't hire anybody not brighter than I am. If they're not brighter than I am, I don't need them."

- Alabama Coach Paul "Bear" Bryant

"Regardless of who was coaching them, they still would have been a great team. I said early in the season that they were the nicest, even sissiest, bunch I ever had. I think they read it, because later on they got unfriendly."

- Coach Bear Bryant on his 1961 Crimson Tide squad.

"But there's one thing about quitters you have to guard against – they are contagious. If one boy goes, the chances are he'll take somebody with him, and you don't want that. So when they would start acting that way, I used to pack them up and get them out, or embarrass them, or do something to turn them around."

- Alabama Coach Paul "Bear" Bryant

"I told them my system was based on the "ant plan," that I'd gotten the idea watching a colony of ants in Africa during the war. A whole bunch of ants working toward a common goal."

- Alabama Coach Paul "Bear" Bryant

"Recruiting is the one thing I hate. I won't do it unless my coaches tell me I've just got to. The whole process is kind of undignified for me and the young man."

- Coach Bear Bryant

"I don't hire anybody not brighter than I am. If they're not brighter than I am, I don't need them."

- Alabama coach Paul "Bear" Bryant

"Sacrifice. Work. Self-discipline. I teach these things, and my boys don't forget them when they leave."

- Alabama Coach Paul "Bear" Bryant

"My approach to the game has been the same at all the places I've been. Vanilla. The sure way. That means, first of all, to win physically. If you got eleven on a field, and they beat the other eleven physically, they'll win. They will start forcing mistakes. They'll win in the fourth quarter."

- Alabama Coach Paul "Bear" Bryant

"If you whoop and holler all the time, the players just get used to it."

- Alabama Coach Paul "Bear" Bryant

"I tell young players who want to be coaches, who think they can put up with all the headaches and heartaches, can you live without it? If you can live without it, don't get in it."

- Alabama Coach Paul "Bear" Bryant

"Find your own picture, your own self in anything that goes bad. It's awfully easy to mouth off at your staff or chew out players, but if it's bad, and you're the head coach, you're responsible. If we have an intercepted pass, I threw it. I'm the head coach. If we get a punt blocked, I caused it. A bad practice, a bad game, it's up to the head coach to assume his responsibility."

- Alabama Coach Paul "Bear" Bryant

"Scout yourself. Have a buddy who coaches scout you."

- Alabama Coach Paul "Bear" Bryant

"But it's still a coach's game. Make no mistake. You start at the top. If you don't have a good one at the top, you don't have a cut dog's chance. If you do, the rest falls into place. You have to have good assistants, and a lot of things, but first you have to have the chairman of the board."

- Alabama Coach Paul "Bear" Bryant

"A good, quick, small team can beat a big, slow team any time."

- Alabama Coach Paul "Bear" Bryant

"I'm no innovator. If anything I'm a stealer, or borrower. I've stolen or borrowed from more people than you can shake a stick at."

- Alabama Coach Paul "Bear" Bryant

"I honestly believe that if you are willing to out-condition the opponent, have confidence in your ability, be more aggressive than your opponent and have a genuine desire for team victory, you will become the national champions. If you have all the above, you will acquire confidence and poise, and you will have those intangibles that win the close ones."

- Alabama Coach Paul "Bear" Bryant

PRAISE FOR THE BEAR

The legendary Hall of Fame coach with the trademark houndstooth hat led the Crimson Tide to six national championships during his career. By the time he retired in 1982, Coach Paul William "Bear" Bear Bryant had more wins than any coach in college football history. More important than all of the victories and championships are the sheer numbers of lives that were touched and continue to be inspired by this near mythological human being with the unforgettable moniker "Bear".

The legacy of Bear Bryant continues to serve as an inspiration for millions of people in Alabama and across the South, as Bryant served as the head coach for three of the 14 Southeastern Conference football teams during his career (Kentucky, Texas A&M and Alabama).

"His nickname was Bear. Now imagine a guy that can carry the nickname Bear."

- Former Alabama Quarterback Joe Namath

"This must be what God looks like."

- Former Kentucky quarterback George Blanda, who played for Coach Bear Bryant at UK, writing about his thoughts upon first meeting the coach.

"I can't imagine being in the Hall of Fame with Coach Bryant. There ought to be two Hall of Fames, one for Coach Bryant and one for everybody else."

- Former Crimson Tide tight end and current Baltimore Ravens GM Ozzie Newsome, upon his induction to the Alabama Hall of Fame.

"We were in the first meeting with Coach Bryant and he told us in four years if we believed in his plan and dedicated ourselves to being the best we could be we would be national champions. He was right."

- Former Alabama All-America guard Billy Neighbors on Coach Bryant's initial address to the team in 1958.

"If I could reach my students like that, I'd teach for nothing."

- An Alabama professor after observing the reactions of players to a pregame talk by Coach Paul W. "Bear" Bryant.

"Bryant can take his and beat yours, and then he can turn around and take yours and beat his."

- Former Houston Oilers coach Bum Phillips, who was an assistant coach at Texas A&M under Coach Bear Bryant in 1958.

"I scored a touchdown on the first reception I made in the NFL and spiked the ball. The instant I did, I felt horrible and couldn't wait for the game to end so I could call Coach Bryant and apologize. He said he didn't even notice, but I never spiked the

ball again."

- Former Alabama and Cleveland Browns Hall of Fame tight end Ozzie Newsome

"I'd do it again in a minute. If you're a football player, you dream of playing for Coach Bryant."

- Former Alabama defensive player John Mitchell, on being the first black player to play football at Alabama.

"He literally knocked the door down. I mean right off its hinges. A policeman came in and asked who knocked the door down, and Coach Bryant said, "I did". The policeman just said "Okay" and walked off."

- Jerry Duncan describing an angry Coach Bear Bryant in the locker room immediately after a 7-7 tie with Tennessee.

"He was simply the best there ever was."

- Nebraska coach Bob Devaney

"He wasn't just a coach. He was the coach."

- USC coach John McKay

"Even his peers in the coaching business felt in awe of him. He had such charisma. He was just a giant figure."

- Penn State coach Joe Paterno

"Coach Bryant has put a lot of people into coaching, but he's put a lot of people out of coaching too."

- Georgia coach Vince Dooley

"I don't know if the Bear is the best coach among us, but he sure causes the most commotion."

- Michigan State coach Duffy Daugherty

"He literally coached himself to death. He was our greatest coach."

- Ohio State head coach Woody Hayes at Bear Bryant's funeral.

"Woody is a great coach . . . and I ain't bad."

- Coach Bear Bryant after Alabama defeated Woody Hayes and the Ohio State Buckeyes 35-6 in the 1978 Sugar Bowl.

"Today we Americans lost a hero who always seemed larger than life. ... Bear Bryant gave his country the gift of a life unsurpassed. In making the impossible seem easy, he lived what we strive to be."

- President of the United States Ronald Reagan describing Bear Bryant's legacy in a statement on January 26, 1983. A month after his death, Coach Bryant was posthumously awarded the Presidential Medal of Freedom, the nation's highest civilian award, by President Reagan.

REFERENCES

"Bob Stoops calls SEC propaganda-driven; Will Muschamp fires back | Gator Bytes blog: University of Florida | The Palm Beach Post." *Blogs | www.palmbeachpost.com*. N.p., n.d. Web. 19 Aug. 2013. <http://blogs.palmbeachpost.com/gatorbytes/2013/05/08/bob-stoops-calls-sec-propaganda-driven->.

"Bobby Bowden Retiring Quotes - Bobby Bowden Retirement Plans." *Esquire*. N.p., 30 Nov. 2009. Web. 19 Aug. 2013. <http://www.esquire.com/features/what-ive-learned/ESQ0901-SEP_WIL>.

Deford, Frank. "Southern Pride And The Southeastern Conference : NPR." *NPR.org*. N.p., 5 Sept. 2013. Web. 19 Aug. 2013. <http://www.npr.org/2012/09/05/160535645/southern-pride-and-the-southeastern-conference>.

"Eddie G. Robinson Museum." *Eddie G. Robinson Museum*. N.p., n.d. Web. 19 Aug. 2013.

Maisel, Ivan. "Game, rivalry couldn't be scripted any better - College Football - ESPN." *ESPN.com*. N.p., 17 Nov. 2006. Web. 19 Aug. 2013. <http://sports.espn.go.com/ncf/columns/story?columnist=maisel_ivan&id=2665659>.

"Manning Family Featured In ESPN Documentary."
OLEMISSSPORTS.COM - OLE MISS Official Athletic Site.
N.p., 17 July 2013. Web. 19 Aug. 2013.

Schwab, Frank. "Brent Musburger, 73, livens up the first half of
BCS title game with comments on AJ McCarron's girlfriend
(VIDEO) | Dr. Saturday." *Yahoo! Sports.* N.p., 7 Jan. 2013.
Web. 3 Aug. 2013.

"Steve Spurrier Book." *SEC Sports Fans are the Best!.* N.p., n.d.
Web. 19 Aug. 2013. <http://www.secsportsfan.com/steve-
spurrier-book.html#ixzz2Zd6hhjVU>.

Travis, Clay. "Charles Barkley Talks Auburn Football, Petrino to
Tigers : Outkick The Coverage." *Home : Outkick The Coverage.*
N.p., n.d. Web. 19 Aug. 2013.
<http://outkickthecoverage.com/charles-barkley-talks-auburn-
football-petrino-to-tigers.php>.

NOTE ON REFERENCES:

Our source material included well over 150 newspapers and
websites. Many websites were used to double check the
accuracy and attribution of these quotes, including ESPN,
CBS Sportsline, Sports Illustrated, and dozens of college
football specific websites. Newspapers included: The New
York Times, Philadelphia Inquirer, Los Angeles Times, The
Wall Street Journal and Knoxville News Sentinel.

Made in the USA
Columbia, SC
04 June 2017